Recycle Your Boss!

99 Ways to put a BAD Boss to GOOD USE.

Recycle Your Boss!

99 Ways to put a BAD Boss to GOOD USE.

by Pat Hucklebee

Andrews and McMeel
A Universal Press Syndicate Company
Kansas City

ISBN: 0-8362-1778-0

Library of Congress Catalog Card Number: 95-60368

ATTENTION: SCHOOLS AND BUSINESSES

Andrews and McMeel books are available at quantity discounts with bulk purchase for educational, business, or sales promotional use. For information, please write to: Special Sales Department, Andrews and McMeel, 4900 Main Street, Kansas City, Missouri 64112.

Recycle Your Boss!

The complete guide
to the creative and most practical
use of dead bosses, supervisors,
managers, directors -- and anyone else
who lorded it over you and made your life a

Living HELL.

Golf Tee

Tire Block

4.

Raw Sewage Sludge Skimmer

Ironing Board

Japanese Water Bridge

Scratching Post

Sushi Table

Plumber's Helper

Store Mannequin

Tackling Dummy

Mile Marker

Camp Canoe

Door Draft Block Thingy

Hollywood Stunt Double

Cutting Board

Dog Drag

Fireplace P₁

Ski Lift

Car Pool Lane Occupant

Shark Bait

Stamp Lick

Garden Marker

Anti-aircraft Target

Rug Beater

Tiki Torch

Tether Ball Pole

Hot Air Balloon Ballast

Sand Tube Weight Thing-a-ma-bob

Sun Block

Mouse Pad

Hammock

Tropical Fish Toy

NASA Deep Space Probe

Lumberjack Log

Oven Mitt

Umpire's Chest Protector

Windshield Sun Shade

Window Squeegee

Kiddie Gate

Tugboat Bumper

Tomato Stake

Tie Rack

Dinner Party Centerpiece

Radiation Shield

Clay Pigeon

Luggage Rack

Fence Post

Diving Board

Pencil Holder

Child Safety Seat

Ottoman

Firing Squad Post

Fire Extinguisher

Putt-Putt Hazard

CaR BRa

Crab Pot Marker

Chimney Sweep Broom

Overhead Projector Stand

Birdhouse

Nuclear Meltdown Plug

Airline Seat Tray

Mailbox

Two Man Luge

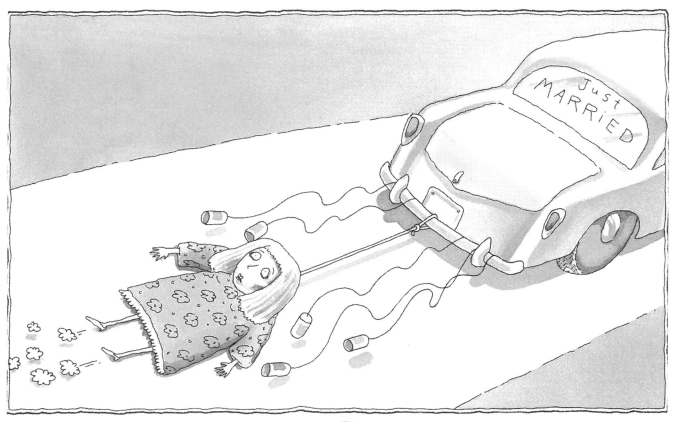

Newlywed Drag Thing

Rodeo Clown Dummy

Tar Mop

Surfboard

Splash Block

Oil Drop Catcher

Drug Bust Battering Ram

Roach Motel

Bungee Tester

Construction Barrel

Garage Sale Sign

Executive Coat Rack

Welcome Mat

Riot Shield

Old West Trail Hider Drag Thing

Easel

Lightning Rod

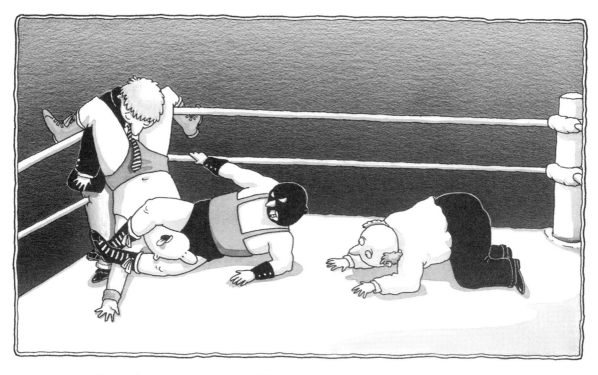

Wrestling Ring Corner Pole

Speed Bump

Marshmallow Toaster Stick

Attic Insulation

Executive Putting Thingy

Hose Caddy

Cane Tester

Merry-Go-Round

Golf Bag

Chamois

Elephant Chew Toy

Demolition Ball

Pool Float

Garden Edging

Book End

Pool Cue

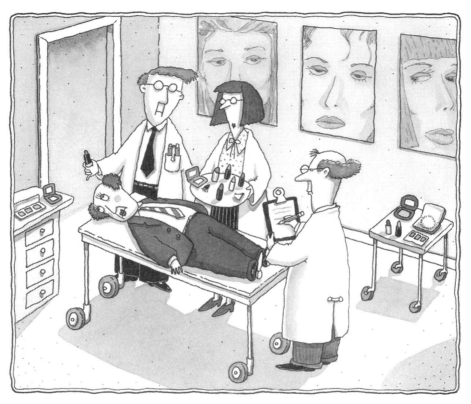

Cosmetic Tester

Surge Protector

And last but
not least,
when all else
fails...